Wake Up, Sleeper!

A Call to the Church

Kathryn Brooks, MEd, LPC

WestBow
P R E S S
A DIVISION OF THOMAS NELSON

WestBow Press books may be ordered through booksellers or by contacting:

WestBow Press
A Division of Thomas Nelson
1663 Liberty Drive
Bloomington, IN 47403
www.westbowpress.com
1-(866) 928-1240

Because of the dynamic nature of the Internet, any web addresses or links contained in this book may have changed since publication and may no longer be valid. The views expressed in this work are solely those of the author and do not necessarily reflect the views of the publisher, and the publisher hereby disclaims any responsibility for them.

Any people depicted in stock imagery provided by Thinkstock are models, and such images are being used for illustrative purposes only.

Certain stock imagery © Thinkstock.

ISBN: 978-1-4497-9035-6 (sc)
ISBN: 978-1-4497-9036-3 (e)

Library of Congress Control Number: 2013905965

Printed in the United States of America.

WestBow Press rev. date: 4/22/2013

TABLE OF CONTENTS

How the Enemy has Gained Spiritual Ground

"I gotta get up; I gotta get goin'"

The words to an old song went through my head as morning beckoned me awake to another day sooner than I wanted. My mid-life body seems to demand more sleep than it did when I was younger. The tumultuous times of each day in the world take more and more of my energy, discipline, and focus to ward off the feelings of anxiety and fear that want to creep into my being. I hear the sounds of the hoof beats of the apocalyptic horses revealed by John the disciple "whom Jesus loved" bearing down on the world with more intensity than ever before. What will the day hold?

Catastrophes litter the news headlines more frequently than the rabbits my husband used to raise. It is almost as if there is a catastrophe de jour, although the end of year highlights from one news program summarized 89 of these major events for the year 2011. As I am writing, military units are building in the Middle East preparing for a showdown. 2013 is already off to a running start of impending dreadfulness.

I see the stupor produced by the constant shock of tragedy that numbs the imagination. Many are simply unable to process the fear produced by such events. I witness the emotional escape even of those who proclaim the name of Christ. The intoxication of the pursuit of worldly values is a too common method to cope, If that isn't effective in sedating the reality, drugs from legal and illegal sources are readily available and gaining acceptability as people become more desensitized to the dangers of these.

I wonder where the evidence of the powerful church of Jesus Christ is hiding. While there is a lot of glitz and show in many mega church platforms, I wonder what is going on where the rubber meets the road, where the common Joe Christian is living. I wonder why many in local congregations appear to be asleep in church services; children, teens and parents are texting on their cell phones during the worship time; and few seem to make the connection between the teachings of scripture and actual day to day life. I wonder why the message of the Good News does not appear to have enough power to attract new generations without gimmicks. Without a doubt, I know the remnant church is still here on earth. In every nation, there are pockets of real Christianity, but frankly, on the bigger scale it looks as if there are greater powers prevailing in the world. The darkness seems to be rapidly getting darker.

When I consider all of these things, even as the day begins, my real concern is what I can do to have any effect on the beloved bride of Jesus Christ during these days. My children and grandchildren are part of that bride, as well as many friends and acquaintances through the years. My one small voice seems very insignificant in a great big world that has many voices blaring constantly through space into vulnerable ears, both young and old. How can I, as part of the bride, shine a light in such a darkening world that it will remind us of hope, truth, and stability? Can I communicate these truths in enough of a profound way that it re-awakens our joy in the midst of these troubled days? Can I address the reality of the negative events in our current world without sugar-coating these; yet, promote more powerful influences that instill a sense of bold confidence and forward looking faith?

I am part of the generation labeled as the Baby Boomers by social science. My generation is moving toward the autumn of its influence; yet, my experience echoes many of the similar experiences of my contemporaries. God has placed me in this time slot in history for the purpose of revealing His glory and if I fail to be obedient to His call, that is my responsibility. There are things to be learned from our experiences and truths to be expressed in the time that we have left. There are no accidents with God, so I must realize that my voice is to be used to point toward Him in these days as much as King David or Queen Esther in their days.

Jesus Christ spoke to such a church in a generation much like mine—the Baby Boomer generation-- when he admonished the church in Laodicea. It was a group of people who had been lulled into a stupor and were not recognizing their condition. In Revelation 3:14-22, he addressed the behaviors that were leading them astray.

> "To the messenger of the church in Laodicea, write: The amen, the witness who is faithful and true, the source of God's creation, says: I know what you have done, that you are neither cold nor hot. I wish you were cold or hot. But since you are lukewarm and not hot or cold, I'm going to spit you out of my mouth. You say, 'I'm rich. I'm wealthy. I don't need anything.' Yet, you do not realize that you are miserable, pitiful, poor, blind, and naked. I advise you: Buy gold purified in fire from me so that you may be rich. Buy white clothes from me. Wear them so that you may keep your shameful, naked body from showing. Buy ointment to put on your eyes so that you may see. I correct and discipline everyone I love. Take this seriously, and change the way you think and act.
>
> *Revelation 3:14–18GW*

In this passage, He warned them of the consequences of their behaviors and prescribed immediate correction and discipline because of his love for them. The paths they were choosing to walk on would bring a rude judgment in the end if they failed to listen to the warning and instructions given to them. However, if they heeded his warning and changed their behavior, Jesus promised the opportunity to share in His victory on His throne for eternity.

Over the next chapters of this book, I hope to awaken members of my generation, as well as subsequent generations, to its call to overcome and be His glorious church for such a time as this The church has an enemy who opposes God and all who belong to Him. The enemy is identified as the devil in the following reference: "Your opponent the devil is prowling around like a roaring lion as he looks for someone to devour." (1 Peter 5:8GW) I will begin by showing at least three tactics the enemy has used to blind and neutralize much of the power of the church in my generation: The enemy has attacked our rest, our sense of safety, and our God-given right of free-will. He has produced an exhausted people, living in denial, and believing every deception that comes along. Jesus confronted similar characteristics as these exhibited in the church at Laodicea as he lovingly, but sternly confronted its condition in his Revelation to the apostle John.

After identifying and discussing the issues at hand, I will also remind believers of the prescription needed in order to recover our passionate belief in a victorious Savior on an individual, as well as on a corporate, level. I will use many of my own personal struggles to demonstrate the tactics that have been aimed at this generation in an attempt to thwart its potential as a witness for God.

Finally, I will include steps to recover what has been lost—a true identity as a valued child of God, chosen in Christ, and destined for victory. God, our heavenly Father, defined a plan throughout history to have a committed relationship with a people who love Him above all other loves. This relationship has the ability to fulfill every true heart's desire and need of our lives. It is a dance of true love. I invite you to join me in this great cause. Time is short and eternal implications are at stake.

The Dance of True Love
By Kathy Brooks

I heard an old tune that triggered a beat
My mind tried to listen to old patterns repeat
Gram cries for treasures now stolen by kin
But offers more access as soon as they grin
Those who would question are put to the side
"You must close your eyes now, continue the ride"
This was our dance of love, my friend
This was our dance of love.

I questioned, as others, and found no relief
The rhythm was strong and the music deceived.
Injustice and pain were just part of the game
Rejection, unfairness, and don't forget shame.
"How dare you to question, our tactics are set…
Your role is to give, and ours is to get."
This was my dance of love, my friend,
This was my dance of love.

Round and round the dance floor we'd go
Stepping in sync with the rhythms of old
Pulling and pushing, then wondering why
Each dance left us empty and ready to cry
Never receiving the love we were told
Would come to us soon if we just fit the mold
This was a dance of love, my friend,
This was a dance of love.

Long seasons were spent on this dance floor of life
To witness sad solos and multiplied strife
Harmonious troops that glide by seemed so fair
Till someone miss-stepped sending all in the air
I'd often been sidelined, rejected and blue
Thinking those dancing were full blessed and true
Deceived by the dance that the world called love
Deceived by the words of false love.

Pain drove me to search the world over to find
A dance of true love of a different kind
The music would play and the partners would call
"Come dance with me now, or you'll miss out on all."
Sometimes I went as the rhythm would draw

Known patterns arose and the hunger would gnaw.
Is there a dance of true love, my friend?
Is there a dance of true love?

Awaking one morning to hear a new song
Strangely fulfilling, yet mindfully wrong
Blood from a cross where a Savior had died
Offering life and love to His bride
"Come dance with Me to the Song of all songs,"
Sung by Moses and Mary; the redeemed from the throng
"Come, dance the dance of true love, my friend."
"Come, dance the dance of true love."

But how could my stumbling feet get in step?
I don't know the moves and am lacking in pep.
My heart was made sick by the long search for hope.
Deceived by false light in the dark I would grope.
"This dance is different," my Lord called my name.
"Give me your heart, trust, it won't be the same."
This is the dance of true love, my child.
This is the dance of true love.

Placing my hand in the nail-scarred hand
We started to move over uncharted land
Ebbing and flowing, the dance drew me so
"My love calms your fears; follow me, and let go."
I know now this dance will last beyond time
Choreographed special to sync with God's rhyme.
This is the dance of His love, my friend,
This is the dance of my love.

I thought once the dance of love could be caught
With songs, dress, and steps from masters who taught
The partners could change, but the dance stayed the same
As ballets reveled in this musical game
Sidelined, alone, my eyes opened to see
For the dance of true love, The Partner's the key
He leads the dance of true love, my friend.
Only He leads the dance of true love.

CHAPTER ONE

"Tactic One – Stealing Our Rest"

You say, 'I'm rich. I'm wealthy. I don't need anything.'
Yet, you do not realize that you are miserable, pitiful,
poor, blind, and naked. Revelation 3:15-17GW

S leep is a surprisingly interesting subject. It has become a topic of scientific research in the past twenty-five years. I became interested in this topic when I developed a condition known as Fibromyalgia after I was involved in a major auto accident twenty years ago.

Pain, muscle spasms, and body temperature irregularities kept me from sleeping many nights. My restlessness also affected my husband's sleep. This fact along with the pain of muscle spasms triggered by simply turning over in the bed caused me to seek how to adjust my sleeping habits. I learned if I turned my body quickly and deliberately, I could avoid the ensuing muscle spasm that would erupt in my legs or back. This movement took my total concentration and control to execute precise timing. My husband experienced this technique as a major earthquake in the bed disturbing his rest as I performed the movement. His patience was challenged many times as he tried to live with me in an understanding way as the Bible admonishes husbands to do.

Nighttime for me became a dreaded place to endure rather than a peaceful place of restoration for the next day. As a young adult, I suddenly felt like a senior citizen. I wasn't ready to give up my physical youthfulness that early. Needless to say, my quality of life in all areas was affected—my family, career, and my faith were challenged. I developed great grief over the loss of the previous physical health I had enjoyed. This health crisis led me to embark on a search for cures to resolve the problem.

Fibromyalgia was not a commonly understood diagnosis at the time and still baffles the medical field. It is characterized by widespread pain with identifiable tender points. I often awoke after a night of fitful sleep and made the statement that "I felt as if I'd been run over by a MACK truck." That was the closest description to what my body was feeling at the time. Imagine my validated surprise when I later found in my research that verbatim statement listed as an identified symptom of the condition on one website.

One of the issues of this condition was the doubt about the reality of my physical perceptions of pain. Pain is not a readily apparent symptom to doctors; something like cancer or a broken bone can be observed under a microscope or on CAT scan. Once a condition is identified and verified, the medical professionals can prescribe a treatment plan because of their previous understanding and research leading to protocols for alleviation of the problem. In my situation, there had been very little research attempted with this condition and the medical field struggled to verify diagnosis and treatment of something they could not see and understand, I struggled along with them and felt like the proverbial guinea pig in an experiment. This process contributed to emotional confusion and distress.

I submitted to rounds of different medical specialists who ordered various tests and prescribed different types of therapies. These ranged from drugs that created havoc in my body to ongoing physical therapies that gave momentary relief but no cure. All of these were very expensive and took a toll on our household budget.

One specialist ordered an EEG (electroencephalogram) and an MRI (magnetic resonance imaging). Following the latter test, my husband and children recall seeing me return home. The neurologist had also prescribed an anti-anxiety drug for which I had no tolerance. Taking the prescribed dosage, I felt the full force of the drug and became totally intoxicated by its effects. I don't recall coming home, or the test, or my husband dressing me following the test. I also don't remember my husband taking me to eat pasta on the way home which he reported to be totally out of character for me and a very funny sight. While this episode gave my family a humorous event to see me under the influence of a drug like that, the test yielded no definitive areas of concern. I chose not to use the drug as a form of escaping the reality of the physical pain, although that option was offered to me.

I wanted to be conscious and able to be an active part of the lives of my children.

I tried to conquer the painful condition by dealing with the psychological aspect to find an answer or cure. I sought psychiatric help for this. Some in the medical community thought that depression was the cause of the disorder, although they really did not know. Medical protocols included prescribing anti-depressant drugs, as well as anti-inflammatory, anti-anxiety, and sometimes drugs to help with sleep. All of these drugs have unwanted side effects, some have been recalled for adverse effects, and some become addictive to patients. None of these therapies was attractive to me.

I agreed with the medical profession that psychological aspects can induce disease processes, but I became convinced that depression was not the cause of this condition. I did not see depression as the root of the disease, thus it would not be the curative factor. In exploring resources available from the counseling field concerning grief and depression; however, I received help to address the grief of losing my health and feeling totally out of control. This cleared much of my confused thinking about myself in this situation and spurred me to take more responsibility for personal management of the condition. I still had ongoing pain affecting my quality of life.

Another avenue I fervently pursued was a spiritual answer, fully believing that God is able to completely heal and restore. In this pursuit, I found myself following a path many others follow. I found myself trying to identify any transgression that would block healing and bring freedom from disease. My quest only contributed to additional frustration and hopelessness as I battled the fact that I just might not have enough faith to bring relief. While I do believe that there may be a strong connection between anxieties (fear) and fibromyalgia which could be resolved spiritually, changing that emotional response and the underlying beliefs supporting anxieties, alone, did not alleviate or remove the physical symptoms of fibromyalgia. Resolving my misunderstanding of God's nature and grace to heal were not the curative factor in gaining relief from this condition

For me, restoration and recovery has been a slow process. It has encompassed growth as a child of God, but it has also required much new learning about health, nutrition, beneficial exercise, and the value of a good night's sleep. Actually, this last factor has been the greatest factor in promoting the physical healing I needed to occur in my body. Restful sleep in sufficient quantity has such benefit to the body that it can change the neurological functioning of the brain, thereby, effecting the physical well-being. Lack of sleep did not necessarily initiate the symptoms of fibromyalgia, but gaining proper rest was integral in bringing about a level of physical recovery. Understanding how to promote that restful sleep in the proper amount was a major key in overcoming the debilitating effects of fibromyalgia in my life.

Like me, a unique population suffers from the effects of fibromyalgia and benefits from current research showing sleep as a major curative factor in this condition. However, according to the U.S. Centers for Disease Control and Prevention (2010), over 25 percent of Americans experience occasional sleep deprivation that leads to physical and emotional symptoms. They can also benefit from a good night's rest. The truth of this modern life phenomenon is exemplified in a more ancient time period in the scripture.

The book of 1 Kings records several events in the life of Elijah, a prophet of God, sent to warn Israel. Elijah confronted the idol worship of the people of God in a contest with the prophets of Baal (the false god) by calling down fire from heaven in a spectacular display on Mt. Carmel. Elijah's favor and success with God led to great threats against his life from the pagan queen, Jezebel. As she threatened to have Elijah killed, he became terrified and ran away. After a day of traveling through the wilderness, Elijah became overwhelmed by physical exhaustion and emotional depression (that happens many times when we don't understand the world's response to spiritual successes). In this situation, God used sleep to help bring healing from the physical and emotional symptoms. 1 Kings 19:5 says "Then he [Elijah] lay down and slept under the broom plant." And again verse 6 repeats the therapy, "So he ate, drank, and went to sleep again." Sleep, as in the case of fibromyalgia, and with Elijah can be the best therapy for overcoming physical and emotional symptoms which affect our mental and spiritual condition. Learning how to get a good night's rest became an important part of my recovery process from debilitating fibromyalgia. Developing ongoing good sleep habits is integral today to maintaining my physical and emotional health.

When I consider the current state of the church, the body of Christ, in the post-modern world today, it appears to me that a large part of it is struggling with symptoms of dis-ease that result in a lot of pain. This struggle is exhibited in the various pursuits of religious hype and deception, disillusionment, alienation from the body of Christ, and an overall lack of peace within individuals, between individuals, and among congregants. As with my experience with fibromyalgia and Elijah's experience with Jezebel, I suggest that some of the symptoms the "body of Christ" displays are actually indicative of a real problem with sleep on more than one dimension. Getting our sleep requirements out of balance can have devastating effects. It can leave us looking as if we are "miserable, pitiful, poor, blind, and naked" as Jesus described the state of the church in Laodicea (Revelation 3:17GW). There is a way to resolve this problem if our condition is acknowledged and addressed directly.

A good night's sleep can do a lot to restore equilibrium as it did with Elijah. The physical rest contributed to his overall well-being. Many people in the body of Christ could benefit greatly from physically slowing down and literally observing the biblical law about the Sabbath Day. Stopping the rat-race for a full 24 hour period each week could have tremendous implications. But Jesus showed an even greater spiritual parallel and application of our need for rest in the gospel according to Matthew. He said the people of the day were not satisfied with Truth but sought to entertain themselves with a show, such as the miracles taking place when Jesus was in town. Jesus had just denounced several cities for refusing to repent and believe in Him although mighty miracles were being done among them. He recognized the true need of the people he was addressing when he offered an invitation to the way of real relationship with God, "Come to me, all who are tired from carrying heavy loads and I will give you rest." (Matthew 11:28GW) He went on to teach that by choosing to get into relationship with Him and align with His vision and work plan, rest would be the result. Jesus actually offers the true rest that affects us spiritually, emotionally, and physically in this passage of scripture. By coming to Jesus, a person can receive eternal life. "...God has given us eternal life, and this life is found in his Son" (1 John 5:11GW). By believing Jesus, Hebrews 4:3 goes on to state "We who believe are entering that place of rest." A place of rest might be perceived like being able to enjoy a good night's sleep—secure, relaxed, peaceful, tranquil and restorative. Jesus invitation to come to Him still holds for each and every person, especially those of his church.

My experience with fibromyalgia has given me some insight into the need for the physical rest God designed us to receive. I experienced the truth of this lesson as I first struggled to sleep with fibromyalgia and then developed better habits which allowed me to experience ongoing restorative sleep. As the Lord dealt with Elijah in his exhausted physical and emotional state, the therapeutic measure of a good night's rest is physical and emotional restoration Spiritual restoration is also available. As a member of the body of Christ, I have learned the value of resting in Christ as He invites the church to do. Taking the first step to fully trust him to provide, lead, succor, and restore goes a long way in boosting my individual being and relationships into the realm of optimum function. It relieves me of striving and brings peace. I believe the first prescriptive step for the restoration of the present-day body of Christ is found in Jesus' invitation, ""Come to me, all who are tired from carrying heavy loads, and I will give you rest. Place my yoke over your shoulders, and learn from me, because I am gentle and humble. Then you will find rest for yourselves." (Matthew 11:28-29GW)

CHAPTER TWO

"Tactic Two – Blinding by Denial"

"You know the times [in which we are living]. It's time for you to wake up. Our salvation is nearer now than when we first became believers." Romans 13:11GW

The National Sleep Institute Project published a list of facts about sleep on the Australian Broadcasting Company in 2000 which included the following:

> It's impossible to tell if someone is really awake without close medical supervision. People can take cat naps with their eyes open without even being aware of it.

This observation is simply interesting trivia at first glance; however, the implications of this researched and documented behavior of people can explain some of the actions of members of the body of Christ in local church congregations. Some people are really asleep even if they appear to be awake and functioning. Any pastor or church leader who has

11

ever spoken in front of a congregation has witnessed this phenomenon. Eyes glaze over and gazes appear to be fixed on something in another dimension as minds wander from the topic at hand. If you have ever driven on a highway and arrived at your destination only to realize that you had been in a daze operating on automatic pilot, you know what the first fact describes. It follows that we can do many activities, some of them potentially dangerous, without having our consciousness fully engaged. The design of the brain must be fantastic, but the ever-present power of God's grace over our existence is awesome if we consider the times He must have protected us in dangerous situations.

Another fact on the list published by the National Sleep Project targeted animal behavior but has implications for human beings.

> Ducks at risk of attack by predators are able to balance the need for sleep and survival, keeping one half of the brain awake while the other slips into sleep mode. (National Sleep Institute Project, 2000.)

This ability occurs in human beings when a person senses danger. The person in danger may possibly be able to sleep; however, he or she may be quickly aroused and prepared to attack if they are feeling threatened. This mechanism is maximized in war zones.

What happens to a person who grows up in a war zone? Can the potentially beneficial use of this ability to survive in a dangerous situation become an obstacle to growing in relationship to God when the person is no longer in the war zone? Can the brain become stuck in semi-alert mode in a deleterious way? Absolutely, it can as has been documented in veterans suffering with Post Traumatic Stress Disorder. This same phenomenon underlies the sleeping church. I believe that many in the body of Christ may be mucking through the Christian life with a less overt block formed under their encounters with stressful situations in the rat race of life. I am referring to a block which creates a half-awareness, but limits the full benefits of life as a Christian.

> Jesus said it like this: You say, 'I'm rich. I'm wealthy. I don't need anything.' Yet, you do not realize that you are miserable, pitiful, poor, blind, and naked. (Revelation 3: 17GW)

As a child born into the second half of the twentieth century, there were several factors that shaped my understanding of the world around me. I was the third (or fourth, depending on who you count) child of parents who had just surpassed their teen-aged years shortly before my birth. I considered myself to have a good home and there were many blessings, but my emotional development in a normal, healthy, fully functional family was inhibited from birth. My parents had married prior to finishing high school and chose to pursue adulthood without the benefit of completing their own individual education and development. They chose to attend the "school of life and hard knocks" instead. Consequently, as adult-children they leaned heavily upon sheer will-power along with some brute power to overcome any obstacles they encountered, including obstacles they encountered from their own children. Their immaturity led them to be abusive in more ways than one to my older brothers as well as myself at times. The trauma of such abuse left its mark on my life, as well as the other children of the family.

Trauma, for my generation, has been an ever-increasingly common event. I was too young to fully understand the political climate of the Cold War or the Bay of Pigs, but the assassination of President John Kennedy was clearly etched in my young memory. As images of JFK's murder and events surrounding it were being televised over the news programs, I became a vicarious witness to the additional murder of his accused assailant which took place in the Dallas police station. These events shocked my child's mind, but adults kept us informed and participating along with their experience of the gruesome chain of events. The ensuing years of my childhood brought additional violence in the United States through news of the Vietnam War, Middle East unrest, racial riots and assassinations of both Martin Luther King, Jr. and Robert Kennedy, witnessed via television camera. Personally, I recall being dismissed early from elementary school in Kansas City due to the threat of rioting in the city. Again, I was too young to process this politically, but I remember feeling fearful. Simultaneously, shopping malls and mega churches were beginning to abound, so distractions were also readily available to take my mind away from the fear.

I could continue with the catalogue of terror and violence I, along with all of my generation have experienced by means of technology until the current day where catastrophes are daily news. While I have been spared some of the direct exposure to many of the national and international disasters, I have been able to experience the horror of these situations via televised accounts and commentaries. Coupled with the sometimes violent outbursts I personally experienced in my own family of origin, I lived in a constant state of fear and anxiety sub-consciously. Traumatic stress became a part of my experience, as it did with most in my generation and beyond, in greater numbers. and more covert ways.

Catastrophic and terroristic events bring us in direct confrontation with the possibility of our own mortality. Faced with constant losses of a sense of safety and hope in the world around me, I began to grieve early in life as I believe many in my generation did. The easily accessible answers available to us were entertainment, materialism, and increasingly glitzy religious prophets that offered more evidence of material blessing than the stinginess and powerlessness practiced at many local churches.

Psychological research which observes and identifies patterns of behavior has produced an understanding of the grieving processes in human beings. The process has specific behaviors, labeled as stages of grief, which a person generally displays as they come to resolve the beliefs and emotions about a loss. Denial is a coping mechanism used during the grieving process. This stage of grief helps shield the individual from experiencing the intensity of the loss too soon before they feel able to do so. It is a protective survival mechanism.

A person can get stuck in the stage of denial. If resources, both internal and external to the person, are not available to draw upon for movement into the final resolution that renders the emotional memories of the loss impotent, a person will remain stuck in denial. The resistance to face the intensely painful emotions may be likened to a child with a physical wound that needs attention, but fights anyone touching it. Others can see the need for attention to the wound, as well as dangers of inattention, but the child fights fervently. Denial is like that resistance and may become a way of life as the person refuses to face the pain of loss and work through to a healthy resolution.

Avoidance of the real issue can become an entrenched behavior pattern. The truth of our mortality produces painful feelings of powerlessness as our vulnerability becomes apparent to us. Because we do not know innately how to deal with that truth, many times we try to live in avoidance or denial of that truth. We seek something or someone more powerful to give us relief from our anxious thoughts. While God and the truth He brings has the most power to bring emotional healing, many, including those in the body of Christ, choose to turn elsewhere and depend upon some form of medication or intoxication to numb the negative feelings and circumvent conscious awareness of truth by stimulating the pleasure centers of the brain. The "medication" chosen to accomplish this result can be anything from alcohol and drugs to shopping, exercise, or even religion apart from a living relationship with the God of the Bible. The goal is to find a way to numb the emotions or distract from the painful feelings. When left to their own devices, people find comfort for the pain much as the wounded child needing more knowledgeable help. Proverbs 14:12 speaks to this dilemma, "There is a way that seems right to a person, but eventually it ends in death." Denial and avoidance is not a good long-term solution to dealing with trauma, the losses produced by trauma and violence, and the grief we feel over those losses.

The Bible warns us as far back as the first of the Ten Commandments not to put anything or anyone else before God, but that is exactly what happens when people pursue attempting to resolve the reality of death and loss apart from God. The pursuit of an ultimately impotent relief mechanism, such as drugs, alcohol, shopping, religion, education, physical prowess, etc. feeds the denial of unresolved fears as it produces the deception of temporary relief. Some people remain in the stage of denial indefinitely only to find that they are locked into an addictive cycle of behavior as they pursue the object of temporary relief with greater commitment. Going deeper into the deception, they become increasingly blind to their real needs

I believe this could be the scenario Jesus addresses in his

clarion call to the church at Laodicea when he confronted them with their obvious denial of their actual state of being. Read the verses again:

> You say, 'I'm rich. I'm wealthy. I don't need anything.'
> Yet, you do not realize that you are miserable, pitiful, poor, blind, and naked. Revelation 3: 17 GW

The verse addresses the statements of denial much like an intervention with an alcoholic. Jesus is talking to the church—those who have professed to believe in Him.

I thank God that my family did attend church because it was at church that I learned about Jesus Christ. However, attending church and learning about Christ and his ways did not immediately erase the coping mechanisms that I had developed as a result of my early home life. There was some relief of pain through the rituals and routines we practiced at church because these were predictable versus the unpredictability of violence and terrorizing events in my private world and the world at large. I simply transferred the denial I used to survive the pain of my family's dysfunction to the church environment. I learned to play the church game well, and could put a Sunday smile on my face with the best of the churchgoers during the late 60's and 70's. Church attendance and involvement, however, did not correlate to daily life. There was a distinct separation between the workaday world and the world of church that represented my understanding of Christianity.

As the modern church became full of people in my generation and beyond who were practicing the same performance-based religion of cultural Christianity, more trauma and violence was experienced as relationships broke down, churches split, and disillusionment reigned when pastors and leaders had affairs or participated in other forms of sexual perversion. The choice for many was to turn away from the church altogether and become devoted to the worldly pursuit of materialism. Others followed different spiritual trends of the time, but found additional deception and disillusionment in many of the reactionary sects. Seemingly, the most powerful demonstration of success in the 80's, 90's and beyond appeared to be the material wealth that flowed through many religious organizations. It mirrored the material success of the whole western world during these decades. Glitz, blinding lights, loud music, and convenient meeting times produced a slick, easy religion that gave enough distraction and salve to anesthetize the emptiness and loneliness of pain momentarily. Consequently, many could say, "I'm rich, I'm wealthy. I don't need anything." (Revelation 3:17 GW) The hope that they could believe the words of televangelists when they instructed them to "believe God" for material blessings became a pursuit of many in the church, even if fiscal evidence was less than convincing.

Jesus confronted this type of church in Laodicea. He is God and has the power to look inside our hearts past the facades we present to the world. In 1 Samuel 16:7, Jesus (the Lord) told the prophet, Samuel, "God does not see as humans see. Humans look at outward appearances, but the Lord looks into the heart." Jesus looks past the wealth and glitz that blinds many and prolongs denial about the true condition of their hearts. He says we have a great need because we are "miserable, pitiful, poor, blind, and naked" (Revelation 3:17 GW) He sees the painful losses of our lives and He sees what we have done to stave off our fears about our vulnerability and mortality. Although, we have come to church and accepted His salvation for our after-life; we are falling far short of the victory He died to give to us in overcoming the world system. The malaise and apathy we experience is the result of our attempts, as the body of Christ, to deny our pain in ways that do not agree with God's word.

Denial has stunted the growth and development of many in the church. It has produced a blinded body that is half asleep in an evil time when we need to be fully awake. "You know the times [in which we are living]. It's time for you to wake up. Our salvation is nearer now than when we first became believers." (Romans 13:11 GW)

I am writing to tell the church of my generation to "Wake Up!" God is gracious and wants us (His Church) to overcome and display His glory. I understood this personally, over a period of time, as I came out of my denial about painful areas I kept from my own consciousness. My self-sufficient pursuits, including participation in religious service, led me to depression, disillusionment, and physical debilitation.

When I recognized my condition and saw the powerlessness of my pursuits, I went back to Christ, the beginning of my salvation. The answer for my restoration, as it is for the whole body of Christ, is found in a real relationship with the Savior. For me, that meant starting at ground zero to learn what being in relationship with Him means. I had tried to relate to Christ out of my own understanding and training as a child, not recognizing those patterns of behavior were serving as a filter to block the truth that is in Christ. In order to follow Christ, we have to be able to hear his teachings.

The first step to recovery and restoration is always acknowledging the issue. Jesus confronted us with His words in Revelation. We can heed his voice and repent (agree with Him and change the way we think and act). This is the easiest and quickest way. However, if we choose to remain in denial of the facts and turn a deaf ear to his voice, God also uses physical circumstances to speak to us. He will speak in such situations as a failing economy or failing health or failing government systems when we realize that we are vulnerable and have a need for His way. We will not arrive in heaven apart from Jesus. He wants us to overcome as He has overcome.

> "I will allow everyone who wins the victory to sit with me on my throne, as I have won the victory and have sat down with my Father on his throne." (Revelation 3:22 GW)

In order to win the victory over fear and other emotional bondages, we, the modern church, must come out of denial and heed the warning to the church at Laodicea as if Jesus was addressing each of us personally. By turning our backs on anything that keeps us from looking to Jesus, we can focus more clearly on Jesus. As the writer to the Hebrews exhorted "… we must get rid of everything that slows us down, especially sin that distracts us. We must run the race that lies ahead of us and never give up. We must focus on Jesus, the source and goal of our faith." (Hebrews 12:2 GW) Whatever is the center of our attention commands our allegiance and wields the greatest influence in our lives. Jesus is the only worthy focus and has bought the right with His own blood to have our full focus and devotion.

We can only develop a relationship with Him as we listen to Him by reading His teachings in the Bible and allowing His living spirit to teach us and guide us. His teachings will call us to obedience to believe Him and follow His ways. He promises the ability to do that as we trust Him. We will face difficult memories as He brings them to our attention and we will find healing in the truth that He shows us. We will continue to face painful situations as evil abounds in the world around us; the writer of Hebrews went on to say, "He (Jesus) saw the joy ahead of him, so he endured death on the cross and ignored the disgrace it brought him. Then he received the highest position in heaven, the one next to the throne of God (Hebrews 12:2 GW).

The promise of Jesus to the believers in Laodicea when they repented and received the remedies for their needs was victory. He validated the words from the writer of Hebrews as well, and extended the opportunity to His bride, the church, when he said, "I will allow everyone who wins the victory to sit with me on my throne, as I have won the victory and have sat down with my Father on his throne:" (Revelation 3:21GW) The rewards are beyond our full comprehension at this point, but the desire of our Savior is that we receive all that He wants to share with us. That is the nature of love and Christ obviously loves His church. It is time to come out of denial about our condition, repent, and receive from Christ

CHAPTER THREE

"Tactic Three – Seeking Full Control"

The end of everything is near. Therefore, practice self-control, and keep your minds clear so that you can pray. 1 Peter 4:7 GW

C risis can be intoxicating to human beings.

Scientific research has shown that nerve centers in the brain command the gates to open for adrenaline and other natural chemicals to flood the bloodstream and push all body systems into peak performance mode ready to respond to the crisis at hand. When this happens, we become single minded in our focus and unaffected by long-term choices and beliefs, able to address the immediate danger to our survival. It is an amazing natural red alert system that prepares us to make the decision to fight or flee in any given situation. After the crisis passes and safety is perceived, the body systems eventually return to a normal functioning state as cortisone is processed out of the system. This response is a natural survival mechanism built into the body of every human being.

As with all things that have been created for good, the possibility exists for this same body response to be used against us. When life is experienced as a series of threats, the effect of this alert process may be likened to a blinking light, stuck in a pattern that continually pumps stimulating chemicals into the bloodstream. With less recovery time between crises, these stimulating chemicals fail to dissipate from the body. A toxic overdose builds up within the body. Some symptoms of this toxic state could be a constant level of anxiety (or lack of peace) and a distorted fearful view of life, as well as physical break-down of organ systems such as the heart and circulation. The potential of harm to the body is great. The inevitable result of the repetitive stress cycle without relief is a condition known as burn-out, a physical and emotional state of utter exhaustion.

Our society is addicted to crisis. The normal activities of my childhood, as with most in my age group, moved at a much slower pace at the start of the last half of the twentieth century than the world moves today. For example, few stores were open on Sundays, pursuit of entertainment was a much lower priority, and relationships, for better or worse, were prioritized and cultivated to a much greater degree. With the advent of screens into the common household, technology brought live news cast of horrific events, cultural influences driven by material acquisition, and ongoing challenges to the once biblically grounded value system of the American culture.

People can recall clearly where they were as they indirectly experienced such traumatic events as the assassinations of JFK, MLK, RFK, as well as violent massacres of students and workers. Coverage of government scandal and brutal celebrity activities were readily viewed by the public. Eyes were glued to screens incredulously viewing the crash of a 747 jet into one of the twin towers in New York City when a second 747 jet crashed into the second tower. Vicarious witnesses stood mesmerized when both towers fell to the ground within the hour. The same process occurred at the explosions of the space shuttles, both Challenger and Columbia. Students watched as a beloved school teacher boarded the Challenger space shuttle, only to witness it vaporize into thin air within a few minutes after lifting off the ground. The Columbia went in a flash of light and explosion that shook northeast Texas and showered remnants from there into Louisiana as it was attempting to return from its voyage. There were video accounts of natural disasters increasing at an exponential rate of occurrence and intensity around the world over this same period of time These are just a few of the shocking events that have been eye witnessed at a distance through the means of technology.

For many, the physical response of viewing these and other critical events over television or other means has been the chemical equivalent of a personal encounter with crisis. Adrenaline flows through the body and produces that single-minded focus that keeps a person glued to the news coverage for hours at a time. In addition, movies, video games, and risk-taking adventures can fill any void of excitement if crisis is lacking. As people experience such common events as road rage in their commutes to work, increasing economic demands, and relational strife, the chemical stimulus remains high producing a "normal" state of crisis. Not having excitement or crisis begins to feel abnormal to many producing symptoms of withdrawal. The physical evidence of this trend is the rising epidemic level of anxiety disorders among those seeking help from medical providers. I believe the culture is moving toward that ultimate physical and emotional burn-out at a rapid pace. And, the church is right in the middle of this procession.

Peter, the apostle, wrote to the church that was experiencing increasing distractions. In 1 Peter 5:7, He encouraged believers to "turn all your anxiety over to God" knowing that the situations they were facing produced a lot of fear and anxiety. Similarly, the writer to the Hebrews encouraged believers to "focus on Jesus" and not be weighed down and distracted by other influences that tend to trip up believers in their spiritual footrace (Hebrews 12:2GW). The ability for mankind to be distracted from God's word, thereby, falling prey to deception and sin goes back to the Garden of Eden. Peter, who had learned his own weakness in the face of crisis when he denied his relationship to Christ, was concerned that believers recognize their susceptibility to falling victim to the enemy's tactics. He instructed the believers to recognize the real battle that was occurring in the spiritual realm. Peter addressed those chosen in Christ who are presently in the world, "Keep your mind clear, and be alert. Your opponent the devil is prowling around like a roaring lion as he looks for someone to devour." (1 Peter 5:8GW) Peter recognized the enemy's attempts to control our minds through deceptive techniques in order to bring bondage and defeat.

These instructions are of infinite value today to the church in the modern world. The enemy is working stealthily as he always has to catch the church off its guard. Even the worldly scientists recognize the methods of mind control that can be used to bring a person into submission. According to an article published in May, 2011 on a website, Science 2020, "mind control refers to a process in which a group or individual 'systematically uses unethically manipulative methods to persuade others to conform to the wishes of the manipulator(s), often to the detriment of the person being manipulated' ". Mind control has been used in hostage situations to brainwash captives into compliance with their captors. The church needs to recognize the same types of methods being used by Satan, the enemy of Christ's church, to distract from the Truth and induce a weakened and demoralized body that is easily defeated from its purpose.

I believe the enemy uses this method of mind control and brain washing through terror to accomplish some of his most prevalent work in the modern church and culture. To terrorize is to coerce by fear or intimidation. Daniel describes a similar effect on God's people when he recorded his vision of the final government before Christ's return. The New Living Translation of the Bible renders Daniel

7:23 with words indicating the intention to wear down the people of God. The enemy uses terror through repeated exposure to crisis and threat of crisis to bring about a gradual wearing down of the church and culture in recent history as people physically and emotionally respond to these crises. Their single-minded concentration on the crisis at hand is a distraction from the real spiritual battle that is attempting to thwart the glorious good news of Christ to be delivered through His church. Satan is using the increasing focus on terrorizing events, natural crisis, and general fears about tomorrow to lead many in the church away from the Prince of Peace. Many, even those in leadership, do not know how to address the falling away directly in an attempt to recover those who are drifting from the Truth.

Again, the purpose of my writing is to challenge the church of my generation and to sound the alarm to "Wake Up" and do the work that we are called to do in our generation. Opportunities are passing our way that will not await our slumbering state. The eternal destiny of people is at stake and blood will be on our hands if we do not sound the alarm to those around us in danger of perishing apart from Christ. The method the enemy is using to control the minds of countless numbers of clueless people is a systematic approach to take captive those who would be saved. The same method has also had an anesthetizing effect on the church. But, we, the church, can recognize the "devil's strategies" as Paul charged the believers at Ephesus (Ephesians 6:11GW). We can choose to be disciplined in our thinking by refusing to be distracted and focusing on the things that are true. As Paul wrote to the Christians at Philippi, "Finally, brothers and sisters, keep your thoughts on whatever is right or deserves praise: things that are true, honorable, fair, pure, acceptable, or commendable." (Philippians 4:8GW) There is plenty in the Holy Bible, God's written communication to us, to fill our minds and help us to know how to live in this present evil world. It is the responsibility of every believer and disciple of Jesus Christ to share the hope of the good news and bring light to the darkness of the evil that abounds. We cannot accomplish this if we are being lulled into a state of apathy.

After sharing the exhortation to not worry about the things on earth by focusing on the true treasures of heaven, Jesus said to his disciples, "Blessed are those servants whom the master finds awake when he comes." (Luke 12:37GW) Peter reiterated the importance of maintaining alertness when he wrote, "Therefore, your minds must be clear and ready for action. Place your confidence completely in what God's kindness will bring you when Jesus Christ appears again." (1 Peter 1:13GW) Obviously, these warnings are given because we need to hear them. We can be distracted and. deceived from fulfilling the plans that God has for each of us. There is great hope in the power of the Good News, but our failure to listen and obey what instructions have been given can keep us from ever experiencing this power in our personal lives. These things ought not to be so for Jesus' church when God has already provided victory.

Hopefully, reader, you are at least pricked in your conscience to consider some of the thoughts that I have put forth in this chapter. If, after you consider these observations, you are not spurred to action, I have missed conveying the urgency of this message. Whether or not Jesus' return is imminent, the time our generation has to serve God will be a limited window of opportunity. As our generation continues to cross the threshold of senior status, the spiritual impact of our generation will be written in the epithets of history. Do we really want to be characterized by the legacy of the church at Laodicea?

I believe there are slumbering saints who have unwittingly fallen prey to the enemy's tactics. These saints hear the warning, but aren't sure how to effectively contend for the faith, as Paul instructed Timothy. You may be one of those saints and need help in knowing the actions that are most helpful in rising up to become all that God desires in these days. There is a path to restoration and victorious living laid out for Christians in the scripture. To help navigate that path, the next few chapters will focus on practical application of scriptural truth to return to Jesus Christ and become obedient to His invitation to the church in Revelation 3:20, "Look, I'm standing at the door and knocking. If anyone listens to my voice and opens the door, I'll come in and we'll eat together." Jesus wants to have fellowship with each one of his followers; he wants to help us gain the nourishment we need to restore our souls so that we may be able to heed his voice. In the previously referenced discourse from Luke 12,

Jesus noted that our hearts (and minds) will be on what we value the most. If we are distracted from the true treasure of God's kingdom by the constant threat of terror from the enemy, the natural result is a waning of the fire and light of the Spirit as we allow His Spirit to be grieved within us and hidden. We are responsible and accountable to Jesus Christ to listen and follow his command to "Be ready for action, and have your lamps burning." (Luke 12:35 GW) We do not know exactly when Christ will return, but for every Christian, we will see Him face to face. Will your lamp be burning when that time comes?

Chapter Four

"Answer the Call-Becoming Fit"

*Examine yourselves to see whether you are still in the
Christian faith. Test yourselves! Don't you recognize that
you are people in whom Jesus Christ lives? Could it be
that you're failing the test? 2 Corinthians 13:5GW*

Tests make a lot of people nervous. Some people get so
nervous that they literally freeze up intellectually and
cannot perform on a test. Many educators have recognized
this obstacle for certain individuals and have made provision
for other ways to measure a student's understanding of a
subject. Success is dependent upon being able to demonstrate
the ability to pass the test. As an educator, in an effort
to remove anxiety about testing, I often tried to prepare
students to understand that the test was only a means to gain
information about how much the student was mastering the
subject. The test was not the final judgment.

I think Paul was trying to make such a point to the
Corinthian believers. They had several struggles with moral
issues in their local congregation that seemed to indicate

that they were not fully aware of what it meant to be a Christian. Paul heard about these situations and confronted the members of this body with the instruction to put them to the test (1 Corinthians 13:3-6). A thorough self-examination could reveal where the real problems in performance lay. As it was for the Corinthian believers, it is imperative for someone who claims to be a Christian to know the basis of their claim in this present time. The final judgment before God's throne will not allow for time to correct and resolve issues discovered, but today's self-examination does allow that opportunity. This present test that Paul prescribes will insure success at the final evaluation before God.

For many in the modern slumbering church who claim the status as Christian, the test Paul recommends is the first step to waking up. Similar to the pre- tests administered in many schools at the beginning of the semester this self-examination will give information about baseline knowledge or the foundational status of the learner. It tells the instructor where instruction needs to begin. The test Paul prescribes is one to know if a person is really in the Christian faith, the absolute essential foundation for any instruction on behavioral expectations. Paul knew that the nature of a being determines its expected behavior patterns. For example, to expect a monkey to act like a pig is unthinkable. A monkey will act like a monkey and a pig will act like a pig, according to each of their innate natures. Paul knew that a true Christian is a new creation of God with a new nature that allows for righteous behavior; whereas, an unbeliever does not have the capability to stop sinning because he is still under the law of sin, separated from God in his nature.

Reader, you must pass this first test before you can hope to grasp and master any other truths about relationship with Christ. This fact, along with an encouragement to mature as a follower of Christ is written about in the first three verses of the sixth chapter of the book of Hebrews. It is important to nail down that time when you made a conscious decision to acknowledge your sinful state of separation from God and to accept His gift of reconciliation through the forgiveness of sins made possible by the death on the cross of Jesus Christ. If you are not freely able to identify that time, or if that time needs to be re-visited at this point, then following Paul's advice to test yourself would be beneficial.

As you test yourself, it may be helpful to consider the attitude Jesus expressed as he entered Jerusalem the final week to face his death upon the cross. He descended into Jerusalem from the Mount of Olives and had a view of the city and its inhabitants. As he saw the people going about their usual behavior, he expressed the very heart of his father, God, when he longingly wished they would allow him to draw them close. He voiced his desire to shield and protect people from their own self-destructiveness in these words recorded in Matthew 23:37, "How often I have wanted to gather your children together as a hen protects her chicks beneath her wings, but you wouldn't let me." Jesus, the very representation of God, the Father, expresses the deep desire to have close relationship with his creation. This same longing was expressed to Adam in the Garden of Eden immediately after the serpent deceived them into listening to his direction instead of heeding the Father's instructions. In Genesis 3:9, "The Lord called to Adam, 'Where are you?'" God came looking for Adam, not because he didn't know where he was, but because God desired for Adam to recognize his separation, the first step to restoration. The heart of the Father is to restore the relationship with his creation.

Adam and Eve failed the very first test of trust and obedience in the Garden of Eden, but God immediately implemented His plan for restoration. It is important to understand the effects of their failure in order to accept the remediation which will give success. Death, or separation from God, was the result of failing that initial test to obey God's instructions concerning the Tree of the Knowledge of Good and Evil. When they listened to the serpent's suggestion that God surely didn't mean to withhold the fruit of that tree from them and wouldn't really impose the death sentence for disobedience even though God had told them so, Adam and Eve set into motion a species of humans who were born spiritually separated from God, or dead spiritually. Their sin created a genetic alteration in their spiritual DNA, so to speak. Genesis records that although Adam had been created in the image of God, Adam and Eve had children born to them in the likeness of their fallen nature, people born separated from God by sin. God's nature is without sin and holy and he cannot have communion with that which is sinful or unholy. In order for God to bring His created human beings back to Himself, He had to put an end to the sin that brought death and separation from His creation. As Paul wrote in the letter to the church at Colossae, "Once you were separated from God. The evil things you did showed your hostile attitude. But now Christ has brought you back to God by dying in his physical body. He did this so that you could come into God's presence without sin, fault, or blame." (Colossians 1:21-22 GW) In a subsequent passage of scripture, Paul wrote, "You were once dead because of your failures and your uncircumcised corrupt nature. But God made you alive with Christ when he forgave all our failures." (Colossians 2:13 GW) God offered the possibility of restoration by sacrificing His very own perfect son, Jesus Christ to pay the debt to God created by mankind's sinful nature.

God did not stop with simply wiping away our sins, Going a step further, He offered a complete restoration of the previously genetically altered spiritual DNA. He replaced our old dead spiritual nature with the very nature of Christ's Holy Spirit, causing us to be born again. Jesus had told this to Nicodemas, a religious leader, when he questioned Jesus about God's kingdom in John 3:3, "Jesus replied, 'I assure you, unless you are born again, you can never see the kingdom of God." In receiving the gift of forgiveness in Christ, we actually receive a completely new nature, a new life, one that is capable of having fellowship with the very God of all creation. Paul wrote it like this,

"Whoever is a believer in Christ is a new creation. The old way of living has disappeared. A new way of living has come into existence." (2 Corinthians 2:17GW)

If you know without a doubt that you have been born again, you have passed the first test that Paul recommended to the Corinthian believers. This is also the first step for the modern church to wake up from its slumber and to return to the Lord's path. A born again Christian is a new creation of God imbued with the power to do God's will. Paul knew this fact of the ability of a saint when he wrote in his letter to the Ephesians, "Don't live like foolish people but live like wise people. Make the most of your opportunities because these are evil days." (Ephesians 5:15-16 GW)

The next step for a born-again Christian is to begin to gain wisdom for life's journey through a growing relationship with Jesus Christ. Studying the scriptures will be most helpful to learn wisdom as long as we prayerfully consider that the goal of all the scriptures is to point to Jesus according to John 5:39 The believer's secret to peace and overcoming victorious power is in knowing Christ himself as Paul wrote in Colossians 2:3 "God has hidden all the treasures of wisdom and knowledge in Christ." As believers in Christ, we have received access to all that is available to us in Christ. For the church of our generation, as we awaken to our status as His followers, we will need to open our ears to hear and our eyes to see the wisdom that is available to us in Christ. We do not want to fail this test of the sincerity of our salvation as the religious leaders of Jesus days on earth. He confronted them face to face, as he later warned the church at Laodicea. His assessment was recorded in Matthew 13:15, "These people have become close-minded and hard of hearing. They have shut their eyes so that their eyes never see. Their ears never hear. Their minds never understand. And they never return to me for healing!" I implore my generation to return completely to Christ, learn to listen to Him, and truly wake up to that entire plan He has for us.

"Wake up, sleeper! Rise from the dead, and Christ will shine on you." (Ephesians 5:13 GW))

Chapter Five

"Overcoming Attacks and Winning the War"

"You are light for the world. A city cannot be hidden when it is located on a hill. No one lights a lamp and puts it under a basket. Instead, everyone who lights a lamp puts it on a lamp stand. Then its light shines on everyone in the house. In the same way let your light shine in front of people. Then they will see the good that you do and praise your Father in heaven. Matthew 5:14-16GW

According to a sales ad on the internet, the world's most powerful flashlight burns with the power of over 4100 lumens and is currently being tested by Guinness World Records. The light beam of this flashlight is so powerful that it can actually ignite a flame similar to a concentrated laser beam. The power of this light is truly a thing of wonder. However, consider the claims of the power of this flashlight in comparison to the claims in scripture about the nature of God, "He is the only one who cannot die. He lives in light that no one can come near. No one has seen him, nor can they see him. Honor and power belong to him forever!" (1Timothy 6:16GW) Paul's words to Timothy reveal something about the magnitude of light in God's presence, a light so blinding that no one can approach. In addition, God's holiness is more powerful than the most robust laser beam man can develop when scripture states that God cannot look on sin because his holy gaze will ignite a consuming fire (Hebrews 12:29GW). With these characteristics in mind, let's explore the power of light in relation to God and His church.

Have you ever been out in the countryside at night away from any light in the city? On a starlit night, the stars are a beautiful sight to behold. With a full moon, the countryside is aglow as if city lights have been activated full force, giving a clear view to walk around without a flashlight. However, in the same countryside, when no light shines, the darkness is palpable. Frightening sounds of nature come alive on every side, but it is impossible to discern the source of the sounds. Without a flashlight, the sense of danger is magnified and safe passage is threatened with every step into blackness. What is clearly visible in the light becomes fearful shadows of impending attack; and, relief from rising terror comes only when reaching a place of refuge.

Light produces a clear view of everything. The apostle Paul stated, "Light exposes the true character of everything because light makes everything easy to see." (Ephesians 5:13-14GW) Paul wrote these words to the church at Ephesus, a place where deception was prevalent within the city and threatening to encroach upon the church. The church at

Ephesus had a lot in common with the present day church of my generation. Deception is so common in the world today that people are beginning to believe that what used to be wrong is right and what used to be right is wrong—a clear example of this trend is the laws that protect certain animal species, while allowing for the killing of unborn human babies. I could continue to list several other examples of what used to be abhorrent to general society that has become tolerated and accepted as normal. But, the point is that deception is as prevalent as it was in the city of Ephesus. If there was ever darkness over a city, it was at Ephesus; and, it is also over our cities today.

The significance of light to the slumbering church is great because it is very difficult to sleep in the light. Anyone who has ever had to work a night shift and attempt to sleep during the daylight hours without benefit of room darkening shades knows the reality of that fact. Jesus spoke to his followers, who were later identified as the church, when he said, "You are the light for the world" to carry the same light that he brought to this dark world."We are his servants because the same God who said that light should shine out of darkness has given us light." (2 Corinthians 4:6GW) Paul also wrote, "Once you lived in the dark, but now the Lord has filled you with light. Live as children who have light." (Ephesians 5:8GW) This idea is repeated to the church in Colossae, "You will also thank the Father, who has made you able to share the light, which is what God's people inherit." (Colossians 1:12GW) With all the availability of light in the church, it seems that sleep would be unnatural, yet warnings have been given several times in this book to "Wake Up". How can the church be asleep in the light?

The Bible has much to say about light. It is the beginning of God's creation in Genesis 1:3, "Then God said, 'Let there be light!' So there was light." The scripture goes on to say that this light was good and that it was separate from the darkness; however, this light was not the creation of the sun, moon, and stars which was recorded in verse 14. The light revealed in verse 3 was connected with the light surrounding God, who is spirit. In this separation from darkness, a reality of the existence of spiritual darkness is validated. From the record of the beginning creation until the return of Jesus Christ as the victorious reigning King of kings in Revelation, light is mentioned in over 230 verses in the Bible. Many of these verses refer to the light connected with God.

If the church is sleeping with all that is written in the scripture about light, can it be possible that the light of many in the slumbering church is really darkness? "If the light in you is darkness, how dark it will be!" (Matthew 6:34GW) The only way to know God and His will is by knowing Jesus Christ and following him. Paul wrote, "God was pleased to have all of himself live in Christ" (Colossians 1:19 GW) and. "God has hidden all the treasures of wisdom and knowledge in Christ." (Colossians 3:6GW) When Jesus came into the world, he said about himself, "I am the light of the world. Whoever follows me will have a life filled with light and will never live in the dark." (John 8:12GW) Thus, any access to "light" other than through a growing relationship to God through Jesus Christ has to be a deception. As Paul wrote in 2 Corinthians 11:14, "And no wonder, even Satan disguises himself as an angel of light." If the church is in the dark and sleeping because of that dark, it has been deceived into that state by the enemy of the church.

Only one remedy is available to resolve this condition. It is to recognize the difference between truth and deception and to become obedient to truth. The remnant church must arouse from its slumber, become alert, and learn to follow Jesus Christ in order to defeat the tactics of the enemy. The wisdom of God is revealed in the life of Jesus Christ and written in the scriptures of the Holy Bible. That wisdom serves as light to see truth, as well as deception. Jesus Christ, who identified himself as I AM, the same as God, came to earth to establish the pathway for each of us to experience a restored relationship with God. As John wrote of what He learned as he walked on earth in relationship with Jesus Christ, "This is the testimony: God has given us **eternal life**, and this **life** is found in his Son." (1 John 5:11GW). John also recorded the words of Jesus in the gospel he authored, "This is eternal life: to know you, the only true God, and Jesus Christ, whom you sent." (John 17:3 GW)

As darkness seeks to blind the eyes of the world, terrorizing people with ever increasing threats, the church holds the light to guide toward refuge. This light is the hope of the Good News that is in Jesus Christ. If we, as the church, know that this hope is living in us, we have the light that the world needs. The light may look like a dying ember in many Christians as the enemy has attacked on every side to keep them from resting in Christ; or, coping with life through denial instead of dealing with issues truthfully and responsibly; or, having their minds controlled through deception that renders them powerless. However, the opportunity to stoke that ember into full flame still remains.

I speak directly to the Boomers of my generation and others who may identify with the state of the church. We can learn to walk daily in the light with Christ in obedience to His word, spending time to read and follow the teachings of the scriptures. As Jesus told the disciples, "Walk while you have light so that darkness won't defeat you. Those who walk in the dark don't know where they're going." (John 12:35 GW) We can also learn to defeat the deceptive manipulations of the enemy who masquerades as light through the weapons God has given us to use because we are sure of our identity as God's born-again child, we are clothed with salvation, righteousness, truth, peace, and we can learn to wield the sword of the spirit, which is the word of God, according to Ephesians 6. We can continue to communicate with God in prayer and expect Him to do all He has promised to do to lead us in overwhelming victory. Paul wrote to the Roman church, "The night is almost over, and the day is near. So we should get rid of the things that belong to the dark and take up the weapons that belong to the light." (Romans 13:12 GW) By God's grace and power, we can wake up and become the glorious church that represents our Savior, Jesus Christ, in the time we have left to do so. We can heed the warnings sounded from scripture by Jesus himself and also from the writer to the Hebrews, "You have come to Jesus, who brings the new promise from God, and to the sprinkled blood that speaks a better message than Abel's. Be careful that you do not refuse to listen when God speaks. Your ancestors didn't escape when they refused to listen to God, who warned them on earth. We certainly won't escape if we turn away from God, who warns us from heaven." (Hebrews 12:24-25GW) This gracious, loving, long-suffering God and Father of all creation has done all to provide for our restoration; but, he also expects us to become alert and obedient to do what is befitting of His royal offspring. Boomer generation and descendents, it is our turn. It is time to truly wake up. As my husband always says, "We're burning daylight!" Let's get going!

"Tactical Summary for Victory"

A s I write this prologue, North Korea threatens to attack the United States, rumors of wars are a daily occurrence, money has suddenly been seized from trusting bank depositors in some European banks, and the stock market just hit its highest level ever without any solid economic evidence to support the rise. The mainstream U.S. media focuses continually on stories that foment fear and threat juxtaposed against the glitz of Hollywood and politics. Threats of imminent danger beside opulent parties and vacations present such an extreme contrast that it is difficult to identify what is true.

With this ongoing media montage that portends doom, most people continue their daily routines as if nothing unusual is occurring even if they have a vague awareness of changes taking place. As long as they can watch their favorite shows on TV and continue to shop at their favorite retail outlets, many members of Christian churches continue to react with the same level of denial. Those who are truly aware of dangers react with confusion, bewilderment, and a sense of impotence. These times remind me of the times Jesus described to his disciples in Matthew when they asked him what the world will be like at the end of the age before His return to earth.

> When the Son of Man comes again, **it will be exactly like the days of Noah. In the days before the flood, people were eating, drinking, and getting married until the day that Noah went into the ship**. They were not aware of what was happening until the flood came and swept all of them away. That is how it will be when the Son of Man comes again. Matthew 24:37-39 GW

Whether or not this is the time immediately preceding the return of Christ, there are very big changes happening in the world around us that are going to affect us. Yet, the masses of the population exhibit many of the behaviors described above by Jesus. A few are aware and awake, but many will be caught by surprise when greater troubles arrive. This trap of surprise can be avoided.

In the previous chapters of this call to awaken, I have attempted to identify the tactics used against all of God's creation to bring chaos, destruction, annihilation, and total separation from the Truth. I have also given the prescription needed to return to God fully to be ready to live in the present and to face the future. By understanding and applying the guidelines covered in the previous chapters, those who are followers of Jesus Christ will be better prepared to recognize and navigate the uncertain times ahead. These points of emphasis are summarized below:

 #1: *Physical rest, as well as spiritual rest, is crucial to our well-being and ability to think clearly to make decisions in the days ahead.*

In chapter 1, I discussed the need for rest to be able to function with robust health. I pointed out that the Holy Bible has examples of the simple need for rest to maintain a proper mental perspective. This was demonstrated in God's provision for Elijah when he ran (1 Kings 19) from the threats of Jezebel. Jesus also confirmed our need to rest in the following invitation: "Come to me, all who are tired from carrying heavy loads, and I will give you rest." Matthew 28:11 GW

 #2: *Denial is only helpful initially to face crisis, but becomes a detrimental coping mechanism in the long run. Being fully alert is necessary to recognize the dangers and to overcome enemy attacks.*

Chapter 2 covered the coping mechanism of denial as a way to avoid the reality of issues we feel powerless to resolve. Ongoing denial is exhibited in avoidance behaviors and addictions. Facing the truth of our vulnerability is crucial to recognize our need to turn to God for help. When we realize how much we are in need, then we will cry out to the God who loves us and has the power to help us during these times. Then, He will help us.

 #3: *Unresolved emotions about trauma can produce a perpetual state of anxiety and arousal that circumvents any rational thinking processes needed to make logical decisions.*

Chapter 3 focused on the effects of stress, not only to our physical bodies, but to our capacity to think and plan. Repeated trauma, whether experienced directly or vicariously, has an anesthetizing effect on the mental capacities of a person when events are not properly processed. The conscious awareness of the event may pass, but the ongoing emotional response remains intact until assertively addressed and resolved. This sub-conscious ongoing experience of the trauma(s) may produce the symptoms of post traumatic stress disorder (PTSD). At the very least, it will produce an ongoing state of arousal and anxiety. Either way, the disorder or the resulting anxiety can interfere with a person's quality of life and ability to manage life decisions optimally. We will need all of our thinking faculties to recognize the increasing deceptions and manipulations being used against us in order to face the challenges ahead.

 #4: *Are you sure you are born again and grounded in the Word of God? You will not be able to stand against the growing tide of evil without the full assurance of God's love and truth.*

In Chapter 4, I encouraged you to do a self-evaluation using the rubric of God's word "...so that your faith would not be based on human wisdom but on God's power." (1 Corinthians 2:5 GW) Wake Up, Sleeper has been written specifically to those who profess to be believers and followers of Jesus Christ and to those who have an interest in becoming a follower of Jesus Christ. Those groups will need more than a casual understanding of salvation to resist the tactics that evil is ramping up against us. We must be sure of our identity as people of God in Christ in order to fully exhibit his nature during the coming days. Jesus Christ will equip each of us to stand in the day of testing through His Word and His Holy Spirit to the glory of the Father.

#5: *Light is a defining characteristic of God and his people, but false light on the earth and in the church is growing in intensity. False light is really darkness.*

In Chapter 5, I attempted to highlight the fact that the true light of God is being imitated by false illumination. The body of Christ has been infiltrated with false teaching and social agendas that masquerade as God's way. While these seem very relevant and palatable to most people, these teachings do nothing to prepare the body of Christ to reject evil and the bondage it brings. On the contrary, these teachings are leading people to vulnerability for any Anti-Christ Savior who might offer answers to many of the world's issues right now. It is important to be able to distinguish between the light of God and the false light of the enemy. We must be aware that we have been warned about this phenomenon from the apostle Paul, "And no wonder, even Satan disguises himself as an **angel of light**." (2 Corinthians 11:14 GW)

In closing this book, I would like to exhort you as a fellow Christian or invite you as a person who is interested in following Christ. These are those days which are fraught with the possibility of great exploits and great defeats. As the battle between good and evil grows ever more distinct,

I hope you will be prepared to take your stand on the side of God's righteousness and His kingdom. The attacks against the body of Christ have already taken a great toll to impoverish many, but God is able to fully save and restore if we will wake up and return to Him. There have been battles and skirmishes that have brought casualties, but the final war is still coming. It is urgent to heed the alarm, arouse from your slumber, get fully dressed and prepare for the battle. You and I are destined for victory.

For this reason, take up all the armor that God supplies. Then you will be able to take a stand during these evil days. Once you have overcome all obstacles, you will be able to stand your ground. Ephesians 6:13 GW

SOURCES CITED

Chapter 1-5

All references to scripture (GW) are from GOD'S WORD. GOD'S WORD is a copyrighted work of God's Word to the Nations. Quotations are used by permission. Copyright 1995 by God's Word to the Nations. All rights reserved.

Centers for Disease Control and Prevention (CDC). Behavioral Risk Factor Surveillance System Survey Data. Atlanta, Georgia: U.S. Department of Health and Human Services, Centers for Disease Control and Prevention, 2010.

"Interesting Facts about Sleep." Compiled by Australia's National Sleep Research Project, 2000.

Maynard, Andrew. "Optogenetics and mind control – on the borders of the plausible?" 2020 SCIENCE.ORG May 8, 2011.